D1128844

IMAGES OF WAR

Blitzkrieg in the West

RARE PHOTOGRAPHS FROM WARTIME ARCHIVES

IAN BAXTER

Pen & Sword
MILITARY

First published in Great Britain in 2010 by
PEN & SWORD MILITARY
An imprint of
Pen & Sword Books Ltd
47 Church Street
Barnsley
South Yorkshire
S70 2AS

Copyright © Ian Baxter, 2010

ISBN 978 1 84884 312 7

The right of Ian Baxter to be identified as Author of this work
has been asserted by him in accordance with the
Copyright, Designs and Patents Act 1988.

A CIP catalogue record for this book is
available from the British Library

*All rights reserved. No part of this book may be reproduced or transmitted
in any form or by any means, electronic or mechanical including photocopying,
recording or by any information storage and retrieval system,
without permission from the Publisher in writing.*

Typeset by Phoenix Typesetting, Auldgirth, Dumfriesshire
Printed and bound in Great Britain by CPI UK

Pen & Sword Books Ltd incorporates the Imprints of
Pen & Sword Aviation, Pen & Sword Family History, Pen & Sword Maritime,
Pen & Sword Military, Wharncliffe Local History, Pen & Sword Select,
Pen & Sword Military Classics, Leo Cooper, Remember When, Seaforth Publishing
and Frontline Publishing

For a complete list of Pen & Sword titles please contact
PEN & SWORD BOOKS LIMITED
47 Church Street, Barnsley, South Yorkshire, S70 2AS, England
E-mail: enquiries@pen-and-sword.co.uk
Website: www.pen-and-sword.co.uk

Contents

Introduction

Blitzkrieg in the West is a highly illustrated record of the German invasion of the Low Countries, and France. The photos with in-depth captions and text presents a unique visual account of one of history's most infamous battles using the tried and tested Blitzkrieg techniques. The story of this lightening campaign vividly reveals how Hitler's war against in the West was won. It shows how the mighty Panzer divisions tore through Belgium, Holland and France, and depicts how these formidable machines accompanied by infantry tore through enemy lines forcing the British Expeditionary Force to withdraw in tatters. The book is an absorbing insight into the German ground forces that played a key part in Blitzkrieg. The reader will find a wealth of information on the vehicles and its components that fought in the campaign. Each chapter brings together a wealth of information on light and main battle tanks, anti-tank guns, assault guns, Flak guns, artillery, reconnaissance units, support vehicles, pioneers with their bridge-building platforms and infantry and Panzergrenadiers. The entire volume is an absorbing read and fully captures all the components that went into making the Blitzkrieg tactics of the early war years such a success.

About The Author

Ian Baxter is a military historian who specialises in German twentieth century military history. He has written more than thirty books including Poland – The Eighteen Day Victory March, Panzers In North Africa, The Ardennes Offensive, The Western Campaign, The 12th SS Panzer-Division Hitlerjugend, The Waffen-SS on the Western Front, The Waffen-SS on the Eastern Front, The Red Army At Stalingrad, Elite German Forces of World War II, Armoured Warfare, German Tanks of War, Blitzkrieg, Panzer-Divisions At War, Hitler's Panzers, German Armoured Vehicles of World War Two, Last Two Years of the Waffen-SS At War, German Soldier Uniforms and Insignia, German Guns of the Third Reich, Defeat to Retreat: The Last Years of the German Army At War 1943 – 1945, Operation Bagration – the destruction of Army Group Centre, German Guns of the Third Reich, Rommel and the Afrika Korps, U-Boat War, and most recently 'the Sixth Army and the Road to Stalingrad'. He has written over one hundred journals including ' Last days of Hitler, Wolf's Lair, Story of the V1 and V2 rocket programme, Secret Aircraft of World War Two, Rommel At Tobruk, Hitler's War With His Generals, Secret British Plans To Assassinate Hitler, SS At Arnhem, Hitlerjugend, Battle Of Caen 1944, Gebirgsjäger At War, Panzer Crews, Hitlerjugend Guerrillas, Last Battles in the East, Battle of Berlin, and many more. He has also reviewed numerous military studies for publication, supplied thousands of photographs and important documents to various publishers and film Production Company's worldwide, and lectures to various schools, colleges and universities throughout the United Kingdom and Southern Ireland.

Chapter One

Preparing for Blitzkrieg

On 9 May 1940 Adolf Hitler finally decided to attack the west and told his Western Front commanders to signal to all units that were preparing to attack across the frontiers of Holland, Belgium and Luxembourg to move to their assembly areas for attack. Later that evening, the codeword, 'Danzig' alerted all German forces that they were to attack in the early hours of 10 May.

The key objective of the attack in the west was the use of the mighty Panzerwaffe units of Army Group A, which were tasked with striking south through Luxembourg and the wooded terrain of the Ardennes which, up to then, had been regarded as impassible for armour. However, Hitler was determined to use the 'old Schilieffen plan' which had been used by the German Army for their attack on France in 1914. In this plan, the German Army placed the main weight of their offensive on the northern wing marching through Belgium. It was here, 26 years later, that the British Expeditionary Force, or BEF, together with the French Army, had expected to meet the main forces of the Wehrmacht. But on the flat lands of Belgium, German commanders were determined that this war of attrition would not be like the dehumanizing years of trench warfare of 1914-18, but would embrace a new concept, as tried and tested in Poland in September 1939 – Blitzkrieg.

Hitler was resolute that if he was going to win the war rapidly in the west the new Blitzkrieg tactic would be instigated quickly and effectively. Whilst he had been aware that his forces had overwhelming superiority in modern equipment against a country like Poland, he knew that France and her allies had a slight advantage in terms of both numbers of troops and material.

Yet, in spite pessimism from many of his Western Front commanders he knew by adopting the Blitzkrieg tactics his army would use highly mobile operations involving the deployment of motorized infantry, air power, and armour in co-ordinated attacks allowing his forces to gain rapid penetration followed by the encirclement of a bewildered and overwhelmed enemy.

For the attack against the west the German Army were divided into three army groups – Army Group A, B and C. The main strike would be given to Army Group A, which would drive its armoured units through the Ardennes, and then swing round across the plains of northern France and then make straight for the Channel coast, thereby cutting the Allied force in half and breaking the main enemy -

Wehrmacht riflemen rest in a field prior to the attack in the west. For the attack against the west the German Army were divided into three army groups – Army Group A, B and C. The main strike would be given to Army Group A, which would drive its armoured units through the Ardennes, and then swing round across the plains of northern France and then make straight for the Channel coast, thereby cutting the Allied force in half and breaking the main enemy concentration in Belgium between Army Group A advancing from the south and Army Group B in the north. The task of Army Group B was to occupy Holland with motorized forces and to prevent the linking up of the Dutch army with Anglo-Belgian force.

concentration in Belgium between Army Group A advancing from the south and Army Group B in the north. The task of Army Group B was to occupy Holland with motorized forces and to prevent the linking up of the Dutch army with Anglo-Belgian force. It was to destroy the Belgian frontier defences by a rapid and powerful attack and throw the enemy back over the line between Antwerp and Namur. The fortress of Antwerp was to be surrounded from the north and east and the fortress of Liege from the north-east and north of the Meuse.

Army Group C, which was the most southern most of the three army groups, was to engage the garrison of the Maginot Line, penetrating it if possible.

Distributed between the three army groups the Germans deployed twenty-nine divisions under Army Group B in the north and forty-four division, including the bulk of the armour, under Army Group A in the centre. Army Group C with seventeen divisions covered the southern flank and threatened the French position on its eastern flank.

Distributed between the three army groups was the armour, which would lead the drive through Belgium, Holland and then into France.In total a staggering 2,072

An officer converses with his staff and a motorcyclist dispatch rider prior to the attack against the Low Countries in early May 1940. Two of the soldiers are wearing the standard pattern model 1935 Greatcoat, which was a long double-breasted item of clothing and when properly worn was designed to reach the wearers calf. The Greatcoat was made of high quality woollen content cloth. The colour of the Greatcoat was a greenish shade of field-grey. It had a deep dark blue-green collar and two rows of six field-grey metal buttons.

tanks. In total there were 640 Pz.Kpfw.I's, 825 Pz.Kpfw.II's, 456 Pz.Kpfw.III's, 366 Pz.Kpfw.IV's, 151 Pz.Kpfw.35(t) and 264 Pz.Kpfw.38(t). The reserves comprised of some 160 vehicles to replace combat losses and 135 Pz.Kpfw.I's and Pz.Kpfw.II's which had been converted into armoured command tanks, which resulted them losing their armament. The vehicles that had been distributed among the ten Panzer divisions were not distributed according to formation of the battles they were supposed to perform. The 1.Panzer-Division, 2.Panzer-Division and 10.Panzer-Division each comprised of 30 Pz.Kpfw.I's, 100 Pz.Kpfw.II's, 90. Pz.Kpfw.III's and 56 Pz.Kpfw.IV's. The 6 Panzer-Division, 7 Panzer-Division and 8 Panzer-Division consisted of 10 Pz.Kpfw.I's, 132 Pz.Kpfw.35(t) or Pz.Kpfw.38(t) and 36 Pz.Kpfw.IV's. A further 19 Pz.Kpfw.35(t) were added to the 6

At a command post and two soldiers are making last minute checks to plans before the Wehrmacht unleashed its mighty force across the border with Holland. The maps and various paperwork can be seen on the table, allowing the men to make any minor adjustments quickly. Not the field telephone on the table, allowing a vital communication link between other command centres and front lines.

Panzer-Division due to the compliment of a battery of sIG mechanized infantry guns. The 3.Panzer-Division, 4.Panzer-Division and 5.Panzer-Division each consisted of 140 Pz.Kpfw.I's, 110 Pz.Kpfw.II's, 50 Pz.Kpfw.III's and 24 Pz.Kpfw.IV's.

In addition to the main armoured force that made up the powerful Panzer division, various other types of armoured units were used. There were for instance four independent Sturmartillerie batteries, each of six Sturmgeschütz (StuG) III assault guns. There was a specially developed vehicle armed with a 7.5cm howitzer bolted on the chassis of a Pz.Kpfw.III. Apart from the new StuG.III there were also two types of independent specialist anti-armour units deployed for action. There were five Panzerjäger companies equipped with a 4.7cm PaK auf Pz.Kpfw.I, which was known as the Marder.I tank destroyer. The vehicle provided at the trim ample mobile anti-tank support for the infantry divisions.

To support the Blitzkrieg there was a single company of ten 8.8cm FlaK 18 auf Zugkrafwagen's. These 8.8cm flak guns were mounted on the chassis of an armoured Sd.Kfz.7 half-track in order to give much needed firepower support against the thickly armoured British Matilda and French Char B tanks.

The Panzerwaffe was undoudbtedly the backbone to Blitzkrieg in the west, and

A decorated commanding officer poses for the camera holding a map board in one hand during the final preparations along the Dutch border. Behind him various vehicles and troops can be seen scattered along a dirt road.

to support its furious drive through the Low Countries and into the French heartlands the Panzers were supported by the infantry divisions.

A typical infantry division in 1940 comprised of the Divisional HQ, which was formed from a Divisional staff Company and a mapping Platoon. The Division itself comprised of three Infantry Regiments which included a reconnaissance Battalion consisting of a mounted Squadron, a bicycle Squadron, an armoured Section, equipped with two Sd.Kfz 221 armoured cars and a heavy Squadron, equipped with three 3.7cm PaK 35/36 anti-tank guns and an infantry gun Platoon equipped with two 7.5cm leIG 18 guns. There was also an artillery regiment comprising of three batteries equipped with four 10.5cm leFH 18 guns and a heavy battalion consisting of three batteries equipped with four 15cm sFH 18 heavy gun howitzers. The bulk of the guns were pulled by animal draught, as most of the towing vehicles were reserved for Panzer and Motorized Divisions. The infantry regiments within the division consisted of three infantry battalions, each formed from three rifle companies. In the rifle companies there existed a machine gun company equipped with eight heavy MG34 machine gun on sustained fire mounts and six 8.cm mortars, and an infantry gun company equipped with two 15cm sIG 33 and six 7.5cm leIG 18 guns.

In order to support the division's drive there was the anti-tank battalion, which

Positioned beneath camouflage netting is a 15cm s.FH18. This weapon was the standard piece in a division and employment of artillery was a necessity to any ground force engaging an enemy. Both infantry and motorized artillery regiments became the backbone of the fighting in the early years of the war.

contained a heavy MG34 machine gun company equipped with twelve 2cm FlaK and three anti-tank gun companies, each equipped with twelve 3.7.cm PaK 35/36 PaK gun.

One of the final supporting elements of the division was the engineer battalion that comprised of three pioneer companies and a motorized bridging Column. The pioneers ensured that division's drive would not be hindered and were always on hand, pending on the speed of the armoured spearhead, to construct pontoons and prefabricated bridges across rivers and canals.

Staff officers during the opening phase against the Low Countries on 10 May 1940. Note the NCO with goggles and holding a map case saluting to his commanding officer. The drive through Holland and Belgium was ferocious and the enemy could do little could to stop the powerful Panzer and infantry divisions achieving their objectives.

A column of motorcycles and motorcycle combinations await orders to advance. Note how the motorcycles are riding in numbered sequence. A six-wheeled Sd.Kfz.231 armoured reconnaissance vehicle passes the halted column. This armoured vehicle was armed with a 2cm gun and an MG34 machine gun for local defence. In the distance an Sd.Kfz.221 light armoured reconnaissance vehicle can be seen, which was armed with just a single MG34 machine gun.

Two officers of Army Group A scrutinize the progress of the their forces during the early operations in the Low Countries. Army Group A, was under the command of Field Marshal Gerd von Rundstedt, and within hours of its initial attack was already advancing through the wooded terrain of the Ardennes.

Panzer officer can be seen sampling the local wine with another office. The Panzer officer wear the new Panzer enlisted mans field cap or *Feldmütze* which was identical to the design and shape of the army officer's field cap and was worn by all ranks. It was black and had the early type national emblem stitched in white on the front on the cap above a woven cockade, which was displayed in the national colours.

A radio operator can be seen about to relay a message. The signalman is operating a portable radio (Tornisterfunkgerat or TornFu). This radio piece was the standard radio system used at battalion and regimental level. These widely used portable radios were carried by a soldier on a specially designed back-pack frame, and when connected to each other (upper and lower valves) via special cables, could be used on the march. The rapid transmission of orders and the fast action taken in response to them were the keys to the success enjoyed by the *Wehrmacht* during the war.

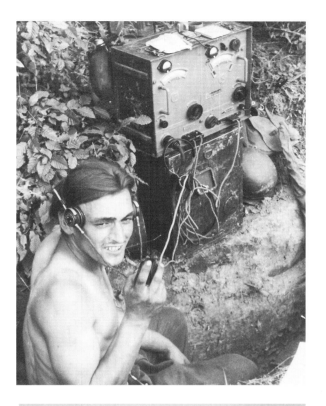

Two Luftwaffe crewmen pose for the camera in front of their halftrack during a pause in their advance through Holland. This vehicle is more than likely towing an 8.8cm Flak gun to the battlefront.

A variety of vehicles and Wehrmacht personnel are seen near a field that has been converted into a makeshift air strip, probably for reconnaissance aircraft. Parked next to the air strip is two six-wheeled Sd.Kfz.231's and two Sd.Kfz.221 light armoured scout cars. In front of the six-wheeled scout vehicle is a camouflaged 8.8cm Flak gun which is more than likely on tow with an artillery tractor. Nearby, stationary on the road is a motor combination laden with supplies seen with its driver next to a PaK35/36 anti-tank gun.

.Panzer commanders confer with the local inhabitants during the German advance through the Low Countries. Behind them is a stationary Sd.Kfz.231 armoured scout car clearly armed with the 2cm automatic canon and a 7.92mm machine gun.

A group of Panzer men, infantrymen and their squad leader armed with the MP38/40 machine pistol stand next to a road full of Pz.Kpfw.III's and other armoured vehicles on their way towards the battlefront. Distributed between the three army groups, which would lead the drive through Belgium, Holland and then into France was 2,072 tanks, 456 of these comprised of the Pz.Kpfw.III.

A Pz.Kpfw.III crosses a stretch of water somewhere in the Ardennes region. Other vehicles in support of the drive can be seen stationary at the water's edge. The key objective of the attack in the west was the use of the mighty Panzerwaffe units of Army Group A, which were tasked with striking south through Luxembourg and the wooded terrain of the Ardennes which, up to then, had been regarded as impassable for armour. However, Hitler was determined to use the 'old Schilieffen plan' which had been used by the German Army for their attack on France in 1914. In this plan, the German Army placed the main weight of their offensive on the northern wing marching through Belgium. It was here, 26 years later, that the British Expeditionary Force, or BEF, together with the French Army, had expected to meet the main forces of the Wehrmacht.

An Sd.Kfz.221 four-wheeled armoured scout car advances along a dusty round bound for the battlefield. Initially this vehicle was manned by a two-man crew and armed with a single 7.92 mm MG34 machine gun. However, the lack of firepower quickly became a major issue and the vehicle had its armament increased. The upper hull structure was re-designed to allow the fitting of a KwK30 2cm Flak Cannon design and built by Rheinmetall along with the existing MG34 to deal with any potential problems encountered on the battle field.

Motorcycle troops of the Lehr-Regiment rest in some woods and tuck into some of their rations during early operations in the Low Countries. The Lehr-Regiment operated in both Belgium and Holland and advanced through France to Paris in mid-June 1940.

Infrantrymen and two motorcyclists with their motorcycle combination have halted at the side of the road and can be seen tucking into their rations. Within hours of the invasion German infantry were already achieving great successes on all fronts against a demoralised enemy that were in already in retreat in many places. Although there was great dependence in the German Army upon the horse for over eighty percent of the motive power, the Germans nonetheless managed to swiftly advance through the Low Countries and overwhelm the enemy with the use of combined aerial and armoured attacks. Along the entire front German forces continued pushing forward using formidable shock tactics by encircling the enemy.

One of the quickest and effective forms of transporting equipment and armour to the front lines was by railway. Here wheeled vehicles are being transported by special flat-bed railway cars to the front. Throughout the war the Germans adopted this type of transport as the quickest method of moving panzer divisions from one part of the sector of the front to another. Whilst it became generally more dangerous by mid-1943, earlier in the war much of the rail transport was moved relatively without hindrance.

Three photographs showing motorcyclist during operations on the Western Front. The motorcyclist is wearing the motorcycle waterproof coat. This coat was issued to members of motorcycle units and individual motorcyclists. The motorcycle waterproof coat was a double-breasted rubberised item of clothing. It was made of cotton twill coated rubber, with watertight seams and the coat was worn over the service uniform. The coat was loose fitting and the ends of the garment could be easily gathered in around the wearer's legs and buttoned into position, which allowed easier and safer movement whilst riding the motorcycle. The motorcycle coat was grey-green in colour and had a woollen field-grey material collar with large pockets. When in use the wearer normally wore the army canvas and leather issue gloves or mittens. Normal leather army boots were often worn. Insignia was not officially worn with the coat, but NCOs and officers were sometimes seen attaching their uniform straps. However, without shoulder straps, which were normally the case, the wearer's rank could seldom be identified. When required, the wearer generally wore his personal equipment over his rubberised coat including the gas mask canister and gas cape. The motorcycle coat was a popular, practical and very durable piece of protective clothing, and was worn throughout the war. It was so popular, that even infantrymen were sometimes seen wearing the coats and had adapted the garment by cutting it short to the knee and removed the wrist straps. Although this allowed ease of movement, it lacked prolonged use and as a consequence the durability of the garment quickly became shabby and torn.

Infantrymen and motorcyclists wearing goggles around their neck pose for the camera. All the men wear the regular army service uniform Model36, which was specifically issued for battlefield conditions. This service uniform was field-grey in colour and manufactured from wool/rayon mixed material. It had four box-pleated pockets with a single metal finish button sewn to each of the four three pocket flaps. There were also five metal buttons sewn down the front of the tunic. The collar of the tunic was faced with dark blue-green material and sewn into this was the German Army collar-patch indicating NCOs and other ranks.

Two motorcyclists and their commanding officer pose for the camera inside a village somewhere on the Western Front. Apart from the shoulder straps and collar patches, one of the most popular and easiest forms of identifying a soldier's rank on his service uniform was the use of a system of arm rank chevrons. The chevrons were normally stitched or embroidered onto a backing cloth of dark blue-green material, but this obviously depended on the type of service uniform being worn. The motorcyclist in this photograph can clearly be seen with a single rank chevron indicating that he holds the rank of an *Oberschütze*.

Supporting the German army's mechanized Blitzkrieg during operations on the Western Front was the Krupp Protze light truck. Popularly known as the 'boxer' due to its air-cooled flat-4 engine, this vehicle provided valuable support for the rapidly moving army by towing artillery pieces and carrying troops and supplies. This particular vehicle is towing a PaK35/36 anti-tank gun. This gun was quite capable of causing some serious damage to its opponent, even though it was not very effective at penetrating thick armour. Whilst it proved its worth of sorts in the West in 1940, a year later on the Easter Front it became an inadequate for operational needs in the face of growing armoured opposition.

Next to a church somewhere on the Western Front and troops pause in their advance. A mobile field kitchen can be seen behind the men. The majority of the soldiers wear the standard M1936 service uniform with the black leather infantry mans belt. Attached to the belt they wear their rifle ammunition pouches.

A Krupp Protze light truck is seen towing a 7.5cm l.IG18 infantry gun. A typical infantry regiment controlled three infantry battalions, an infantry gun company with six 7.5cm l.IG18 and two 15cm s.IG33 guns, and an anti-tank company with twelve 3.7cm PaK35/36 guns.

A Pz.Kpfw.IV Ausf.D probably attached to the Lehr-Regiment during operations on the Western Front. For the battle against the West there were some 366 Pz.Kpfw.IV's that saw operations. Originally the panzer was designed as an infantry support weapon, but by the end of the campaign in the West the tank had proved to be so diverse and effective that it earned a unique tactical role on the battlefield.

An Sd.Kfz.231 in the field. This vehicle was armed with a 2cm KwK 30 L/55 automatic cannon, and a *Maschinengewehr* 13 machine gun. It had a second driver in the rear so that the vehicle could be driven either forwards or backwards. The 231 was introduced into service in 1932 and began to be replaced in 1937 when the German Army switched production to 8-wheeled armoured cars instead of 6-wheeled. Despite being replaced, they were used by reconnaissance units (*Aufklärungs*) during operations in Poland, the Low Countries, France and then during the early part of the war on the Eastern Front.

A Pz.Kpfw.II advancing through a field. Both in Poland and on the Western Front the new tried and tested Blitzkrieg strategy of warfare owed much to the German light tanks, in spite them being intended primarily for training and light reconnaissance work.

An Sd.Kfz.221 moving across a field. This light armoured vehicle had well sloped armour and small open top machine gun turret. Later variants had the turret fitted with mesh wire covers for protection against hand grenade and shrapnel and was armed initially with the 7.92cm MG13. Later models were armed with the 7.92cm MG34 machine gun.

A 7.5cm l.IG18 infantry gun with crew. Each infantry regiment possessed its own artillery in the form of 7.5cm l.IG18 and 15cm s.IG33 infantry guns, which were regarded the workhorse pieces operated by specially trained infantrymen. Each infantry gun company had six 7.5cm l.IG18's.

Moving across a bridge infantry can be seen manhandling an artillery battery's limber that is attached to a 10.5cm howitzer. Note the provisions stored on the limber including a bale of straw for the horses to feed and logs in order to prevent the guns wheels sinking in soft ground.

Infantry with their horses on the Western Front. Much of the supplies during the early part of the war were transported by animal draught. Even during the campaign in 1940 commanders in the field found that quite frequently the panzers outstripped their supplies that were being transported by horse which consequently temporarily hindered movement. It would not be until the war on the Eastern Front that this problem became much worse with larger distances to travel.

A column of halftracks stationary beside a road. By 1940 the halftrack had become a necessity on the battlefield. With the bulk of the Wehrmacht still relying heavily of animal draught the Germans used the halftrack extensively not only to tow ordinance and other supplies, but to carry troops to the forward edge of the battlefield.

A convoy pauses on a road and soldiers can be seen dismounting from their infantry trucks more than likely to take up positions before continuing their drive. Whilst the majority of troops marched on foot, support vehicle were available to transport infantry and supplies to the front lines.

A view in this photograph depicts the 15cm howitzer being towed by a prime mover. The 15cm howitzer was the standard heavy field gun in the Wehrmacht. It was very effective at clearing up heavy concentrated positions to let tanks and infantry pour through unhindered.

A Junker 52 transport aircraft seen on an improvised air strip somewhere in the Low Countries in May 1940. The JU52 was primarily used to transport supplies quickly to ground troops in the field. It was also widely used to transport German paratroopers to key targets.

A column of Pz.Kpfw.38(t)'s advance along a road towards the battlefield. This light Czech built tank became the most widely used and important light tank incorporated by the Panzertruppe during the early years of the war. For the campaign against the West there were some 264 of these machines distributed between some of the most powerful panzers divisions.

A long column of support vehicles carrying infantry and supplies. A motorcycle combination passes the column on its way to the front. Note the 'WL' on the vehicles license plate indicating that it belongs to the Luftwaffe. The white lines on the vehicles mudguards are the trucks width markings.

Motorcycle troops, probably from a motorcycle rifle or reconnaissance battalion passes a destroyed vehicle as it enters a captured village somewhere on the Western Front. The motorcyclist can be seen wearing the one-piece rubberized waterproof suit. The troops called this garment the *Kradmantel*.

A halftrack towing a PaK35/36 anti-tank gun descends a hill. The PaK35/36 became the standard anti-tank gun of the German Army during the early part of the war. It weighed only 432kg (952.5lb) and had a sloping splinter shield. The gun fired a solid shot round at a muzzle velocity of 762m/s (2500ft/s) to a maximum range of 4025m (13200ft).

Infantry have halted next to a church during a pause in the march. A motorcycle combination is stationary beside an An Sd.Kfz.231 armoured scout car, Sd.kfz.263 radio vehicle, and an Sd.Kfz.221. The Sd.Kfz.263 was not intended to be used for fighting and armament was restricted to an MG34 mounted in the superstructure front. The long-range radio set was accommodated by the provision of a large frame antenna. Of interest note the letter 'K' painted in white or yellow on the front of the vehicles superstructure, including the motorcycle combination. The 'K' indicates that these vehicles belong to *Panzergruppe* Kleist's 1.Panzer-Army.

A long column of support vehicles have halted on a road. Infantrymen pose for the camera. Divisional transport in a typical Panzer division in 1940 amounted to some 452 motorcycles and 452 light and 1133 heavy lorries. Each division relied heavily on wheeled transport in order to supply the armoured spearheads quickly and effectively.

A battery of 10.5cm le.FH18 howitzers in their firing position in a field being readied for action. Normally there were four guns in a battery, but sometimes pending on losses or the strength of the enemy the battery was occasionally consolidated into slightly larger batteries. Note the special wicker cases for the projectiles. A number of the projectiles have already been primed by the crew for firing.

A 5-ton Sd.Kfz.6 medium halftrack can be seen towing a 10.5cm le.FH18 howitzer across a pontoon bridge. In total, the 10.5cm howitzer had either an eight or nine-man crew, and can be seen on the bridge and inside the halftrack.

Commanding officers pose for the camera whilst standing inside their command vehicle overseeing operations in the West. Behind them in a field are other vehicles including a motorcycle and a halftrack towing a PaK35/36 anti-tank gun and a full complement of crew. Note the divisional insignia painted in yellow on the side of the command vehicle indicating that it belongs to the 3.Panzer-Division.

Soldiers can be seen preparing to unload supplies in a newly captured position on the Western Front. Despite the huge logistical problems that faced the Wehrmacht during their drive, the support vehicles were relatively successful at maintaining momentum.

A 15cm howitzer is being towed by animal draught. The gun was broken down into two loads, each drawn by six horses. In this photograph the carriage and mounting are camouflaged with saplings. The gun's tube and breach were transported on a special four-wheeled wagon.

Following a units march Gebirgsjäger troops have set-up camp. A group of soldiers have contributed their shelter-quarters to assemble a functional tent. By the appearance of this position the troops have been here some time and even constructed a small makeshift fence around the tent with local wood.

Chapter Two

Battles of Holland and Belgium

Early on 10 May 1940, the invasion of the Low Countries finally began. Initial air strikes paralysed enemy defences along the Dutch and Belgium frontier. Minutes later, *Fallschirmjager* (paratroopers) began massive glider and parachute assaults with a series of key objectives. In total 12,000 troops from the German Airborne Division were assigned with the tasks of attacking and securing key airfields and bridges around cities such as Rotterdam, Amsterdam, Utrecht, and Dordrecht.

In Belgium the Fallschirmjager received a number of immense and risky challenges which not only included the destruction of a string of heavily armoured

An Sd.Kfz.263 radio vehicle. This radio vehicle (*Funkspähwagen*) was equipped with extra long-range radio equipment and an additional radio operator. To support the additional equipment, the turret was omitted, the superstructure was raised, and only a single ball-mounted machinegun was mounted.

fortifications along the frontier, but one of the most formidable fortifications in the world, the one at Eben Emael. Whilst its forces unleashed a maelstrom of fire against the huge bunker system in Belgium, other key areas in Holland were also be obtained by the elite German paratroopers. Despite the fact that the Dutch forces had been forewarned of an invasion and stiff resistance was encountered, the Fallschirmjager skill of deployment and battle tactics captured all its objectives. Over the city of Rotterdam, bewildered inhabitants watched in horror as German paratroopers landed in the football stadium, and then advanced at breakneck speed to capture the Meuse bridge. The Morediik and Dordrecht bridges were captured intact and held in the face of heavy resistance until German ground forces arrived.

Whilst the Luftwaffe wreaked death and destruction across both Belgium and Holland and the Fallschirmjager fought to hold key objectives, German ground forces at first light began striking across the frontier. Army Group A, under the command of Field Marshal Gerd von Rundstedt, were already advancing through the wooded terrain of the Ardennes. Through the narrow twisting lanes, between slopes and over many humpbacked bridges, cut by streams which in some places were unfordable, columns of Panzers and motorized vehicles rattled across Belgium, Luxembourg and French borders. Out of the 10 Panzer divisions, seven

A column of vehicles from an unidentified unit stationary on a congested road. On one side of the road infantry can be seen in a number of wheeled vehicles including a Krupp Protze light truck. Halted alongside these vehicles is a Pz.Kpfw.I, a tank destroyer which was basically a 4.7cm PaK(t) built on the chassis of a Pz.Kpfw.I, and behind that is an Sd.Kfz.251 halftrack.

A unit crosses border control into France observed by bewildered French civilians. Note the Czechoslovakian-made steel hedgehog anti-tank obstacles that have been cleared out of the way for traffic.

of these were directed through the mountainous wooded countryside of the Ardennes, supporting General Heinz Guderian's force. Rolling through villages, tank men from open turrets smiled and waved to amazed civilians. The roads they used were more a matter of traffic control rather than actual fighting, and one breakdown of one large vehicle might have been enough to bring the invasion in the south to a standstill. But the flat land beyond was tank commander's dream. With wide open plains, Panzers would be able to make a grand sweep through France northwards towards the Channel coast, thus cutting the Anglo-French armies in two.

Whilst Rundstedt's force advanced westward, meeting hardly any opposition, in the north, General Fedor von Bock's Army Group B crashed over the Belgian and Dutch borders. As these unprecedented forces drove on, village by village, town by town, thousands of Fallschirmjager and land glider-borne troops were landing on airfields, bridges and fortified posts in order to create a clear path for armour and motorized infantry.

By the end of the first day of Blitzkrieg, Belgian resistance had been over-whelmed and the cavalry of the French 9th Army brushed aside. Although the

French 7th Army had reached Breda on 11 May by the next day it was in retreat under strong pressure from Guderian's Panzers. By evening of that same day, the Panzer units reached the Meuse along a 100-mile front, from Sedan to Dinant. They had advanced nearly 90-miles in three days. As the whole front began to crumble in indecision and confusion, the demoralized French Army tended to its wounds and withdrew to Antwerp along roads clogged with refugees. To the south, French troops immobilized in the Maginot Line were unable to move for the lack of transport, and were clearly unable to intervene against strong German forces.

The Belgian Army too were falling victim to this rapid German advance. Because they had suffered such appalling casualties, they were streaming back in their thousands to the BEF's defence line.

Through the retreating column that littered almost every main road, Belgian troops outnumbered the exodus of refugees. Much of the Belgian artillery was pulled by horses or mules, and many wounded were carried on carts. The picture was one of a defeated army trying in vain to escape the impending slaughter.

Elsewhere along the front lines the situation was equally as grim. Dutch troops had tried to hold their meager positions against overwhelming forces but were

A bicycle unit supported by motorcycles cross the French border following in the wake of the furious advance of the armoured spearheads. By the appearance of the damaged brick wall the French have put-up some degree of resistance.

slowly and systematically battered into submission by the German Blitzkrieg tactics.

By 15 May, the Dutch Army formally surrendered, although isolated units continued to fight a grim defensive battle until 17 May. As German troop occupied Holland with lightening speed, Belgium's capital finally capitulated. A potential disaster now loomed as in 1914, but the crises this time was much worse. Confusion was sweeping the BEF's front lines. Shortages were everywhere and in everything. A critical lack of transport soon confronted the troops, and roads busy with refugees made large-scale troop movements almost impossible. Soon many units became trapped, captured, overrun, and slaughtered. The British were now seriously confronted by the fear of losing their only army, and entire parts of their air force if they continued to stand by their Allies on a collapsing battle line. The French too were under incredible pressure from the German onslaught, and foresaw their army breaking in two, with the stronger part falling victim to the encirclement in Belgium and areas in the north. It was now decided in order to save their forces from complete destruction the BEF would have to make a fighting withdrawal into northern France and hopefully stave off a catastrophe there.

Along the same wall as in photo on page 39 and Wehrmacht troops can be seen marching into France. Three infantry regiment made-up the division's main fire and maneuver elements. Their objective was for two infantry regiments to take ground, whilst the other remained in reserve.

Two photographs showing Junkers Ju 87 or *Stuka* (from *Sturzkampfflugzeug*, 'dive bomber') leaving an airfield for a bombing mission against BEF forces. The Stuka had made its name during the campaign against Poland and became an integral part of Blitzkrieg tactics in 1940.

A long column of horses towing 10.5cm howitzers accompanied by artillery crew's march along a road destined for the front lines. Above in the sky two Ju52 transport aircraft can be identified.

A 10.5cm howitzer battery can be seen advancing across a field. Note the splinter shield protected by a shelter-quarter. The 10.5cm howitzer had a good reputation on the battlefield. It was a reliable and stable weapon and crews found it easy to maneuver from one part of the front to another.

Two photographs showing infantry crossing a river with motorcycles and bicycles on an improvised ferry. Part of a pontoon bridge has been lashed across pneumatic boats and a soldier can be seen with one of the boats paddles guiding across the river. This type of improvisation was common and the pneumatic boats were capable of relatively large loads.

A motorcyclist leads an advance of a column as it passes through a barrier in Belgium. By the state of the barrier it appears that the gates have been blown open by demolition charges allowing German forces to push on through.

Inside a French village and a PaK35/36 crew stealthily edge their way forward towards enemy fire. Of interest note how the crew has utilized obsolete ammunition boxes and attached them on the guns splinter shield. Also, note a dismounted cyclist observing a dead comrade laying face down on the pavement, evidently caught in fighting with the enemy.

A light cross-country staff car approaches a badly damaged bridge. The bridge had more than likely been bombed by Luftwaffe aircraft as its forces attempted to cut off withdrawing French, Dutch, Belgian and British forces.

A typical scene on the Western Front in May 1940 showing one of the many congested road systems. A variety of vehicles can be seen on the road comprising prime movers towing 15cm howitzers, light four wheeled vehicles and infantry trucks.

A nice view of a 15cm sFH 18 heavy field howitzer horizontal sliding breechblock. The crew can be seen standing with the gun, probably awaiting orders to put this deadly weapon into action.

Two photographs showing a camouflaged 21cm Mrs18 with gun carriage concealed in a field with crew. This heavy mortar large-calibre gun had a range of almost 17 km, the large calibre and its enormously effective fire made the mortar a very effective artillery weapon. Although it was hindered by its weight of some 16.7 tons it remained in service until the end of the war. It was widely used destroying enemy fortifications and well dug-in positions.

A 17cm or 21cm artillery gun is being towed by an 18-ton Sd.Kfz.9. Foliage has been applied to the gun and its carriage in an attempt to break-up its distinctive shape. The size of the gun can be compared to the passing female civilian refugee pushing a pram on the cobbled road.

An interesting close-up view of a 95.7-pound 15cm sFH 18 high-explosive projectile. The explosive has been removed from its wicker container and sits on a special mat waiting to be placed into the guns breechblock.

A photograph taken the moment a projectile leaves the gun tube of a 21cm K-39. Note how some of the crew members plug their ears as the massive blast reverberates the position. The protective wicker cases for the ammunition can be seen to the left of the photograph.

Hurtling along a road towards the front lines is a 8-ton Sd.Kfz.7 medium halftrack towing a well camouflaged 15cm sFH 18 heavy field howitzer. During the campaign in the West the halftrack transformed the fighting quality of the artillery batteries and enabled gun crews to support the advancing armoured spearheads with less difficulty than using animal draught.

During a pause in the advance and infantry and field kitchen personnel pose for the camera beside a shell hole. Behind them a HF 12 small kitchen wagon can be seen. These could operate on the move, cooking stews, soups, and coffee. The limber carried utensils and equipment. The troops nicknamed these kitchen wagons as 'goulash cannon's'.

The crew of a 15cm s.FH18 unlimbering the gun from its limber in order to prepare the weapon for firing. Note the letter 'C' painted on the guns limber indicating the position of the gun in the battery.

A 10.5ch light field howitzer has been set-up in a field near a French village. The projectiles are stacked up in readiness for firing. One of the crew members sits near the projectiles with paperwork.

A variety of vehicles including a light Horch cross country vehicle, motorcycle combinations, and a Krupp Protze light truck can be seen at a traffic control point near a pontoon bridge. The sign is redirecting traffic to a 16-ton bridge.

Two photographs showing an unidentified artillery battery moving along a road with horse drawn transport towing limbers and caissons. For the immediate needs of battle, the mighty Panzer divisions had required that the artillery arm was composed mainly of vehicle traction. However, even by the time the Wehrmacht attacked the West in 1940 much of the artillery was still being moved from one part of the front to another by horse drawn transport.

Six photographs showing various pontoon bridges that have been erected across the many rivers that stretched through the Low Countries and north eastern France. First engineers would position the pontoon boats (either inflatable or 50-foot pontoon boats) in place and then the bridging equipment would be erected across it in a surprisingly short time. Some of the pontoon boats were fitted with large outboard motors to hold the bridge sections in place against the often strong currents. However, because there were so many waterways that needed to be crossed by so many different divisions the Germans found that they were running out of bridging equipment.

Horse drawn wagons advance a long a dusty road comprising of captured French PoWs. The French soldiers appear to be unnerved by their capture and can be seen smiling for the camera.

A 10.5cm infantry gun crew during a firing mission against an enemy target. On the Western Front the German infantry artillery formed the main organic support of the division and supported the combat troops prior and during action. It was paramount importance that these infantry field guns used on the battlefield were light and maneuverable. The 10.5cm light infantry gun was the ideal weapon for action on the front lines and undertook sterling service against the BEF forces.

A Kfz 21 heavy cross-country car passes through a burning town somewhere on the Western Front. The letter 'K' painted either in white or yellow on the vehicles mudguard indicates it belongs to *Panzergruppe* Kleist's 1.Panzer-Army.

Advancing through a captured town is an Sd.Kfz.251/1 following an Sd.Kfz.10 light halftrack. Note the divisional insignia painted on the rear of the Sd.Kfz.251 indicating that it belongs to the 1.Panzer-Division.

A column of armoured vehicles comprising of the 15cm sIG33 heavy infantry gun and a number of halftracks line the road beside a row of houses in north eastern France. The sIG33 formed the heavy infantry gun platoon of a Panzergrenadier regiment and was well suited for warfare on the Western Front. The letter 'E' and the tactical numbers '706' indicates that this vehicle is the 4th gun of the self-propelled Heavy Infantry Gun Company 706, which belonged to the 10.Panzer-Division. It was part of *Panzergruppe* Kleist's 1.Panzer-Army.

Vehicles belonging to the 1.Panzer-Division are strategically spaced-out across a field to pose minimal threat by enemy aerial attack. The armoured vehicle halted near a light Horch cross-country vehicle is an identified as an Sd.Kfz.10 light halftrack.

Support vehicles cross a pre-fabricated bridge over a flowing river. A Bussing-NAG transport vehicle can be seen towing a 5-ton trailer full of supplies. These fixed-type bridges allowed a constant flow of traffic to cross quickly and effectively without hindered movement.

A dispatcher rider hands a piece of paper containing important information to a member of the signals unit. Signals units possessed more specialized vehicles than any other type of unit in a division.

Two photographs showing horse drawn infantry halted inside a village. The soldiers are more than likely part of a divisional artillery regiment which was organized into four battalions, each referred to as an 'Abteilung'.

Infantry march through a destroyed town, probably in north east France in May 1940. Note the soldier carrying a tube charge, which was known in the West as a Bangalore torpedo. The planks of wood that are being carried were used as the demolition blocks, which were wired to the wood.

A congested road somewhere on the Western Front in 1940. These armoured vehicles belong to the 1.Panzer-Division and comprise of Sd.Kfz.251 halftracks and a StuG.III Ausf.A, which was making its debut on the battlefield that summer. In the battle of France the StuG.III was primarily designed to support and fight alongside the infantry and keep pace with the swift advances of Blitzkrieg. Of particular interest note the letter 'G' on the halftracks headlamp indicating Guderian's XIX.Panzer Corps.

Two photographs showing various vehicles including trucks laden with infantry and supplies crossing a fixed-type and pontoon bridge. Because of the lack of vehicles in the *Wehrmacht* the Germans commandeered a number of foreign vehicles in order to bolster the numbers of wheeled transport.

Stationary Sd.Kfz.251/1 halftracks can be seen parked at the side of the road whilst French PoWs trudge passed. Note the vehicles tactical symbols on the rear. One of the symbols identifies it as belonging to a Panzer unit.

A pioneer truck passes a cordoned off bomb crater more than likely dropped a Luftwaffe bomber. The size of the crater was caused probably by a 1000-kilogram bomb.

An RAF fighter has been shot down over Belgium and lies in a field still burning. The BEF contingent was made-up of nearly 500 RAF aircraft, but many were lost as a result of strong Luftwaffe opposition and extensive German flak battery positions.

A German soldier converses with a Swiss border control soldier on the French-Swiss frontier. The Swiss soldier distinctively wears the M1918 helmet and is armed with the M1911 rifle.

An Sd.Kfz.231 reconnaissance vehicle crosses a field. By the time the Germans invaded in the West the Wehrmacht had more than 600 armoured cars, enough to distribute some 50 or more to each armoured division for reconnaissance duties.

Luftwaffe troops converse outside a captured building adorned with the German national flag. A halftrack with its roof camouflaged with straw and towing a trailer with straw is stationary in front of the building.

A well camouflaged Luftwaffe halftrack travels through a town towing, what appears to be an 8.8cm FlaK gun. The 8.8cm FlaK gun was a very deadly and effective piece of weaponry and scored sizable hits both in an anti-aircraft and against ground targets as well.

A well concealed 7.5cm l.IG18 in a field prior to going into action. Each infantry regiment possessed its own artillery in the form of 7.5cm l.IG18 and 15cm s.IG33 infantry guns, which were regarded the workhorse pieces operated by specially trained infantrymen. Each infantry gun company had six 7.5cm l.IG18's.

A commanding officer receives a lift in a motorcycle combination along a congested road. Whilst a number of motorcyclists during the early war years of the war still road into battle and dismounted to fight, they were also given other duties to perform such communication and reconnaissance duties.

A halftrack advances along a road towing what appears to be a PaK35/36 anti-tank gun. A long column of French PoWs can be seen being marched to the rear where they would be contained in hastily erected prisoner compounds.

Pz.Kpfw.I tank destroyer armed with a 4.7cm PaK(t) advances along a road. This armoured vehicle is attached to the Panzerjäger-Abteilung 570 and has just a railway line near the canal between Pommeroeul and Hensies.

A column of horse drawn transport towing 15cm howitzers towards the battlefront. Note the gun tube and breech of the 15cm howitzer is seen on its transport wagon. The 15cm howitzer was primarily designed to attack targets deeper in the enemy's rear. This included command posts, reserve units, assembly areas, and logistics facilities.

A common sight during the German invasion of the West was the amount of bridges destroyed. Here two photographs vividly portray the extent of damage to two different bridges. In the top photo pioneers have set to work clearing a path to the river bank in order to construct either a pontoon or fixed-type bridge.

German infantry come across the carnage wrought to a French column as it retreated across the Belgium border into France. A horse towing a wagon lies dead among a pile of supplies littering the road. As the Germans advanced across the Low Countries into France sights like this became a common occurrence.

An infantryman in a foxhole poses for the camera. Behind him is a stationary Kfz21 heavy cross-country car. The soldier is wearing the standard M1936 service uniform, which has been unbuttoned due to the heat of the summer day. The German national emblem of an eagle with outstretched wings clutching in its claws a wreath containing a swastika can be seen positioned on the right breast of the service tunic.

Three photographs showing French PoWs along with captured colonial troops are escorted along a road to the rear. Although their German captors treated most French soldiers humanely, colonial troops were not so lucky. When colonial soldiers surrendered they were often humiliated or beaten by German soldiers for putting up a fanatical resistance. However, the Waffen-SS, like the Totenkopf (Death Head) treated them more harshly and frequently took no prisoners, preferring to round up the North African troops and have them summarily shot on the spot.

Adolf Hitler is seen here in Belgium with some of his commanders. As General Kleist's panzers rattled and rumbled victoriously through northern France toward the Channel, on 17 May Hitler left his new Western Front headquarters called 'Felsennest', and motored to the Bastogne deep in the Ardennes to discuss the progress of the main drive to the Channel with the commander of Army Group A, General von Rundstedt. Before driving back to the headquarters Hitler stayed for lunch and later made an appearance in front of an army unit, appearing exhilarated by the success of his troops. However, upon his return to 'Felsennest' he became anxious about reports of undefeated forces in France. It was not until 20 May that he finally reassured himself that the situation was mastered. That evening during a conference he received a communiqué that panzers had arrived at the Channel coast. Success was now only a matter of time. Within three days armoured and mechanized divisions of Army Group A had pushed north, closing the Channel ports of Calais and Dunkirk, whose capture would prevent the British from a sea retreat to England.

Chapter Three

Road to Dunkirk

By 18 May the 5th Panzer Division reported that it had reached the northern bank of the Sambre. Here armoured vehicles from Panzer-Regiment.31 began expanding their bridgehead north of the river. The 28.Infantry-Division pushed further west meeting spirited French resistance.

On other parts of the front the advance was progressing equally as well. General Heinz Guderian's reconnaissance had successfully crossed the River Somme and captured Peronne. Panzers swept on into France, even stopping to fill up at public petrol stations when they outstripped supply facilities. Masses of troops that had not already been killed or injured were persuaded to surrender by nothing more than shouting ordered from the turrets of passing tanks. Once, when several French tanks were captured, General Erwin Rommel, commander of the 7th

A PaK crew with their 7.5cm l.IG18 firing at an enemy target. This weapon was one of the first post World War One guns to be issued to the Wehrmacht and later the Waffen-SS. The gun was light and robust and employed a shotgun breech action.

This page and opposite: Eight photographs showing Waffen-SS troops in action on the Western Front. These troops belonged to the famous 'Das Reich' Division. In 1940 these troops were known as the SS-Verfügungstruppe (Special Disposal Troop). On the evening of the 22 May 1940, the SS-Verfügungs Division proceeded with the 6th and 8th Panzer Divisions toward the port of Calais in order to help strengthen German positions west and south of the Dunkirk perimeter. It seemed that Dunkirk would soon be captured but on the night of 26 May Hitler rescinded his famous 'halt order' and 'Germania' and 'Der Führer' of the SS-Verfügungs Division surged back into action and fought a bloody battle in the de-Nieppe forest. The remaining infantry regiment, 'Deutschland', which was temporarily attached to the 3rd Panzer Division, took part in the attack against British units on the Lys Canal near Merville where the SS troop met spirited resistance.

Panzer-Division, incorporated them into his own column, still with their French drivers.

Karl von Stackelberg, a war correspondent accompanying the rapid German advance, watched with astonishment the pitiful demoralization of the French troops marching to meet them: *'There were finally 20,000 men, who were here...in this one sector and on this one day, were heading backward as prisoners. Unwillingly one had to think of Poland and the scenes there. It was inexplicable. How was it possible that, after this first major battle on French territory, after this victory on the Meuse, this gigantic consequence should follow? How was it possible these French soldiers with their officers, so completely downcast, so completely demoralized, would allow themselves to go more or less voluntarily into imprisonment?'*

Not all French soldiers, under the pulverizing effects of Blitzkrieg, would surrender so easily. In areas north of the country, they resisted steadily, until finally the French 1st Army and the BEF were constricted between the North Sea and the advancing German armour.

By 20 May, after racing north along the Somme against fierce resistance from

Three photographs showing infantry and artillery crossing a river. Two of the photographs show a column of vehicles, infantry and a 15cm heavy field howitzer crossing over a heavy pontoon bridge (Brückengerat B) and light pontoon bridge (Brückengerat C). One of the photographs showing a 15cn sFH heavy field howitzer being towed by an 8-ton Sd.Kfz.7 medium halftrack.

the British 12th and 23rd (Territorial) Divisions, the first Panzers came in sight of the Channel coast. In no more than 11 days, Guderian and his force had advanced 400 miles and done what the German Army failed to accomplish in four years of during the First World War. It seemed nothing on earth could stop this stampede of military might from crushing the Anglo-French troops that were being driven along the Channel coast. But, as plans were put forward by Guderian to move his 10th Panzer Division on the port of Dunkirk, where it was believed there was a considerable number of isolated enemy troops, General Edward von Kleist, removed Guderian's 10th Panzer. Guderian was ordered to capture Boulogne instead with the 2nd Panzer Division, and his 1st Panzer Division attack Calais.

By nightfall of 22 May, Guderian's 2nd Panzer Division, after a drive of more than 40 miles, was on the outskirts of Boulogne. In the town itself, the British commander, Brigadier William Fox-Pitt, had orders to defend Boulogne 'to the last man and last round'. While he organized a hurried defence in the hills, which surrounded the port, British troops, under a storm of heavy concentrated fire, were being dramatically evacuated from the port by British warships. As German troops closed in to secure the port, panic-stricken British soldiers fled and attempted to rush one of the last ships to leave the harbour. Further up the coast,

French and British soldiers have been captured and can be seen standing in a village whilst German horse drawn infantry with supplies pass by.

Two officers pose for the camera in front of a destroyed Pz.Kpfw.35(t). For the invasion of the West the Panzer divisions mustered a total of 151 Pz.Kpfw.35(t)s. Although these light tanks were thinly armoured they operated with much success in 1940 in spite being susceptible to anti-tank fire.

in the battered town of Calais, the situation of the BEF was equally dire. The bravery shown by the British 30th Brigade to defend the town was said by attacking German troops to a '*useless sacrifice*'.

As disaster loomed in France for the entire Anglo-French armies it was becoming clear to the British that their hopes would rest entirely on the port of Dunkirk, and its beaches. Here, the wide, flat, featureless sandy shoreline, surrounded by heavily contoured dunes and tufted with marram grass, stretched some 25-miles from Gravelines in the west through Malo-les-Bains, Bray Dunes and La Panne to Nieuport, a few miles across the Belgian frontier in the east. Behind the dunes, house fringed the sand, and field beyond them stretching to the horizon were cut by canals and irrigation ditches. Because there was no cover, and the surrounding fields had been flooded, the area was regarded as particularly different country for armour.

For a number of days, thousands of exhausted, disheveled troops with a large assortment of vehicles, ranging from armoured cars to ambulances, swarmed through Dunkirk and on to the beach. Relations in Dunkirk between the Allies were already strained. The British were more concerned about evacuation, but the French regarded the port as a fortress, a base in which to launch the counter-attack which would somehow undermine the German thrust into France.

Three photographs showing the extent of destruction to some of the towns in north eastern France. The BEF often put-up heroic resistance in the face of overwhelming superiority, but the Germans eager to push forward their armoured spearheads frequently subjected many towns and villages to merciless heavy artillery bombardment and aerial attack.

Already Dunkirk was in shambles. All along the beach, signs of devastation were everywhere. German gunners had already positioned their 15cm heavy artillery howitzers outside the town and were sporadically pounding the town and its beaches. Inside the bombed and blasted town, a swirling mass of despondent men, horses and guns clogged the streets leading to the beach. Thousands of British, French and Belgian soldiers crammed into the dwindling perimeter around the town, hoping that evacuation from the sea would arrive at any moment.

As the BEF waited to be evacuated, Guderian's 1.Panzer-Division, which was racing towards Dunkirk, reached Aa Canal between Holque and the coast and secured bridgeheads across it. On 24 May, with just a few miles to cover before reaching Dunkirk, the General received a startling *'Führer Order'*: *'To halt commencement of operations towards Dunkirk'*. The tanks were stand west of the canal line, and the Luftwaffe was given the task of breaking all resistance from the encircled enemy and prevent any British forces from escaping across the Channel. Guderian wrote, 'I was utterly speechless. But since we were not informed of the reasons for this order, it was difficult to argue against it'. Many other divisional commanders were equally amazed at the halt order. But one such commander

Taking cover behind a wall are infantry accompanied by two signalmen that can be seen carrying the Torn.Fu.b1 backpack radio. The signals battalion provided both field and radio communications support within the division, linking all subordinate units.

'Sepp' Dietrich, was so outraged that in total defiance he ordered Hitler's foremost fighting unit, the SS-Leibstandarte Adolf Hitler (LAH), to cross the Aa Canal to fight its way into Watten. He was latter taken to task for his disobedience.

Outside Dunkirk, other bewildered commanders found it hard to come to terms with the order. With their panzer divisions growling no more than a matter of miles from the town's outskirts, they knew very well they could capture it with littler trouble. However, there had been widespread feeling of uncertainty in the German High Command of committing the Panzers into what Hitler remembered from his own experiences of the First World War, '*as the marshy plains of Flanders*'. But as Manstein later outlined, Hitler's decision was probably due to the fact that he was eager to keep his armour intact for the coming battle in central France, and that Goring deserved the chance to use his Luftwaffe to smash the BEF on the beaches.

A group of infantrymen prepare for operations inside a French town. They wear the M1935 steel helmet in the standard matt slate-grey finish. They have been issued with the standard M1936 field blouse. The soldiers are armed with the usual rifleman's equipment; the army enlisted mans leather belt, rifle ammunition pouches, bread bag, field flask with drinking cup, mess kit, shelter quarters and gasmask in its M1938 metal canister.

Infantry on horseback examine an abandoned Hotchkiss H1939 tank. This French tank was used widely against German forces in the West and some 550 were captured in France and used by the Germans as the Panzerkampfwagen 35H 734(f) or Panzerkampfwagen 38H 735(f), which were mainly for occupation duty.

A motorcycle unit with sidecar combination has halted on a congested road. On the Western Front each Panzer division had a very capable motorcycle company. In fact, a whole battalion of a Panzer division's rifle brigade were given motorcycles with sidecar combinations.

On a congested road and a bicycle unit can be seen keeping to one side of the road as they pass a long column of fleeing refugees. Movement for infantry was often hindered by civilian traffic and it was frequently easier in some areas to leave the road and advance across country. However, bicycles were compelled to keep the road as uneven surfaces caused a number of problems, especially with punctures.

An infantryman and a motorcyclist examine an abandoned Char DI heavy tank. This French tank only saw limited action on the Western Front and made no real impact even against the light Pz.Kpfw.I.

Advancing through France towards the battlefront is a Krupp-Protze Kfz.69 truck towing a 3.7cm PaK 35/36 anti-tank gun. To the left of the photo two officers can be seen conversing, one with a map in his hand.

A group of infantrymen stand beside a column of captured French soldiers. The German troops are outfitted with the M1936 field uniform with a field grey tunic and M1935 steel helmet. They wear the stone grey trousers and high-topped leather marching boots. For armament they carry the Mauser 7.9mm Kar98k carbine, the standard issue Wehrmacht's shoulder weapon. One soldier, probably a troop leader, is armed with the MP38/40 machine pistol.

French troops have just surrendered to a German unit. The German attack through France was swift and effective and the French forces were shocked by the speed and fire power of their enemy.

A General can be seen reviewing operation plans during the invasion of France in May 1940. Pinned to his General's tunic he displays a Knight's Cross of the Iron Cross.

Inside a French town and 2cm FlaK gun has taken-up a position. Once the gun was unlimbered and leveled by three adjustable feet, the gun layer could then climb into the seat and prepare the weapon for action. Note the guns two-wheel trailer nearby.

Two photographs showing a French Renault R35 tank has been knocked out of action evidently from a heavy anti-tank mine. The R35 equipped 21 battalions, each of 45 vehicles. In total there were some 900 allocated at Army level. Losses on the Western Front were immense.

Pioneers with their bridge building sections inside a decimated town. The column includes halftracks with Horch cross-country cars towing bridge equipment 'T' Type pontoon trailers.

A halftrack can be seen pulling part of the ordnance of an 18 or 21cm Morser along a congested road. In order to support the doctrine of Blitzkrieg the Germans widely used halftrack vehicles primarily designed move artillery to the forward edge of the battlefield quickly and effectively.

A Pz.Kpfw.III, motorcycle combination, a light Horch-cross country car and a supply truck are seen on a road not far from Dunkirk in late May 1940.

A well concealed Pz.Kpfw.I in undergrowth. During the Western campaign it soon became apparent in tank versus tank combat of the deficiency of the Pz.Kpfw.I. However, fortunately for the Wehrmacht the light Panzers had succeeded destroying the bulk of the enemy armour using tried and tested Blitzkrieg techniques.

An interesting photograph showing captured British soldiers being transported to the rear onboard a Pz.Kpfw.I outside Dunkirk in May 1940. Around the Dunkirk perimeter German troops were eagerly trying to prevent the last of the BEF forces from escaping onto the beach.

Infantry and crew stand on and around a Pz.Kpfw.38(t). Logs have been festooned on the rear of the engine deck in order to prevent the vehicle from sinking in soft ground. This light tank undertook sterling service in the Western Campaign Panzer crews and mechanics found the vehicle relatively reliable and easy to work with.

A photograph showing two French Renault R35 tanks abandoned next to a German staff car. Many vehicles in the BEF were simply overrun by the rapid thrust of the German spearheads and the crews literally had no time to withdraw their machines to another defence lines. Another problem the BEF were faced-with was the lack of fuel as supply lines had either been severed due heavy fighting or cut-off by surrounding

Two German infantrymen examine a knocked out British Vickers Mk VI light tank. The British Royal Armoured Corps divisional cavalry regiment was each equipped with twenty-eight Mk IVs, whilst the 1st Armoured Division, was equipped with 257 tanks, of which a large number were Mk VIB and Mk VICs. The 3rd Royal Tank Regiment, which formed part of the division's 3rd Armoured Brigade, possessed twenty-one Mk VI light tanks.

Children can be seen examining a stationary Pz.Kpfw.I inside a destroyed town in northern France. By the extent of damage to the buildings the town has been subjected to heavy aerial bombardment.

Two photographs, one showing pioneers attacking a French fortification and the other of a captured French bunker installation outside Dunkirk. These fortifications were often heavily defended and were frequently put out of action by determined German assault pioneers. Pioneer troops were mainly employed as assault troops to supplement the infantry. Their task involved clearing minefields, breached obstacles and attacked fortifications with demolitions and flamethrowers.

A German supply truck towing a trailer is seen in front of a burning building. In the cobbled square some of the furniture from the destroyed building has been salvaged by the inhabitants.

A column of motorcyclists accompanied by a variety of other vehicles move through a destroyed town in northern France. The BEF that attempted to defend these towns against the German spearheads were often subjected to merciless heavy aerial bombardment, reducing some of the towns to rubble.

Outside Dunkirk and vehicles can be seen burning. On 27 May, the Luftwaffe took to the sky and destroyed Dunkirk with successive waves of bombers, accompanied by fighter escorts, which pulverized the town and the harbour. Whilst the Luftwaffe attacked Dunkirk and its beaches the Germans attempted to hold back the last remaining enemy forces escaping to the coast.

A photograph taken along the coast at Dunkirk following its capture. A soldier holding the rank of *Spiess* (RSM or 1st Sergeant) converses with his commanding officer. Destroyed vehicles and equipment are strewn along the road in front of the damaged buildings.

A German photographer takes a poignant image of a British grave as a grim reminder of the sacrifice the BEF forces suffered on the beaches of Dunkirk. With little to defend themselves most of the troops were exposed to the constant bombing raids by the Luftwaffe, and as a result many were killed.

Chapter Four

'Operation Red'
Blitzkrieg through France

On the ground the German drive through France was undertaken effectively and efficiently. In the air the Luftwaffe continued attacking selected targets, mainly going for enemy troop concentrations and bridges. The sudden surprise attack; the bombers and fighter planes soaring overhead, reconnoitering, attacking, spreading fire and fear; the Stukas howling as they dived pounded the BEF troops as they mercilessly tried to claw their way back through France to the Channel Coast. In a number of areas German tank commanders reported that the enemy was simply brushed aside, thrown in complete confusion. In the most cases the defenders lacked any force capable of mounting a strong coordinated counter-attack. British artillery eager to stem the tide of the German onslaught, poured a storm of fire into advancing German columns, but they soon found that the Germans were too strong to be brought to a halt for any appreciable length of time. In some areas the Germans found the quality of their opposition extraordinary and uneven. At one moment a handful of them were receiving wholesale enemy surrenders, at the next, an entire division was being held up by stubborn resistance of a company of French or British troops with a detachment of artillery and anti-tank guns. However, British and French commanders struggled desperately to hold their forces together. They were paralyzed by developments they had not faintly expected, and could not organize their forces in the utter confusion that ensued on the battlefield. In a number of areas the virtual collapse of the communication system had left many commands isolated, making it difficult for them to establish contact with the fronts. Consequently decisions were almost invariably late and therefore disastrously overtaken by events of one position after another being lost to the Germans. The BEF, however, tried to regain the initiative to the last man and last round, even when they had long since been over-taxed, but coupled with the ineffectiveness of their troops, significantly reduced by the destruction transport, an ultimate catastrophe now threatened the British and French Army.

Already the fleeing BEF troops were being mauled almost to death by constant air and ground bombardments. In the confusion and mayhem that engulfed the British and French lines, the troops were struggling to hold back the finest fighting army the world had ever seen. The quality of the German weapons, above all the tanks, was immense importance to Blitzkrieg. Their tactics were the best; stubborn defence, concentrated local firepower from machine-guns and mortars, rapid counter-attacks to recover lost ground. German units often fought on even when cut off, which was not a mark of fanaticism, but great tactical discipline. The invasion of the Low Countries and France was a product of great organization and staff work, and marvelous technical ingenuity. Everything it seemed went according to plan, or even better than the plan in the unfolding both of strategy and tactics. Both Hitler and his staff were confounded by the lightning speed and the extent of their own gains. The overwhelming German air power was decisive to the strategy and this enabled troops to operate with almost total freedom from enemy interferences. Many captured British soldiers complained bitterly about difficulties caused by aircraft and its material damage upon formations in transit. Almost all were indeed seriously delayed by the harassment upon the roads and by the wrecked river and railway bridges. Yet, for airmen that fought in the skies

Horse drawn wagons are seen here crossing over a heavy pontoon bridge known technically by the German pioneers that erected them as a Bruckengerat B. Note the 50-foot long pontoon bridges fitted with large outboard motors in order to hold the bridge in place against the strong river current.

over France, ground attack was regarded as infinitely hazardous. Like all low-level bombing, it required unrelenting concentration and precision. These operations inflicted immense damage upon the BEF, but not without the loss to aircraft.

Whilst the Luftwaffe continued to roar over head causing devastation in its wake the German ground offensive through France relentlessly pushed forward. On 24 May 1940, the German objective was to annihilate the British, French and Belgian forces which were surrounded in Artois and Flanders, by a concentric attack by the German northern flank and by the swift seizure of the Channel coast in the area. The Luftwaffe was to break all enemy resistance of the surrounded forces, to prevent the escape of English troops across the Channel, and to protect the southern flank of Army Group A.

However, with the panzers halter outside Dunkirk it allowed the British and a substantial part of the French 1st Army to reach the water sanctuary of the 'Canal Line'. When the panzers were finally revoked to move once more on 26 May much of the BEF had escaped onto the beaches. The following morning on 27 May, the Luftwaffe took to the sky and destroyed Dunkirk with successive waves of

Following the mighty panzers in the rear were usually horse drawn supplies seen here crossing a Bruckengerat C bridge accompanied by some infantry on foot. The pontoon boats were normally fastened both ends and bridging deck sections secured over them.

An interesting photograph showing a horse drawn supply convoy halted in a field. Among the various wagons and limbers is a HF 12 small kitchen wagon. Whilst Blitzkrieg in the West was notably very successful for the Germans supplying the advanced elements of the armoured spearheads were often slow in arriving. Much of this was owed to the Wehrmacht still not being fully mechanized, relying mainly on animal draught to try and catch up the main body of the advancing forces.

bombers, accompanied by fighter escorts, which pulverized the town and the harbor.

Whilst the Luftwaffe attacked Dunkirk and its beaches the Germans attempted to hold back enemy forces escaping to the coast. On 28 May, General Erwin Rommel's 7.Panzer-Division captured Lille, trapping half of the French First Army and preventing their retreat to Dunkirk.

But in spite fervent attempts by the Germans to prevent the escape of the BEF, every vessel that could cross the English Channel fearlessly sailed into Dunkirk, braving some of the most appalling conditions to rescue the soldiers marooned on the beaches.

By 4 June some 337,000 Allied soldiers had been saved from capture. The majority of the 110,000 French troops after arriving in England were transshipped immediately and returned to the French ports in Normandy and Brittany to rejoin the rest of the French Army that were gallantly trying to defend northern France from the clutches of the German military might.

There now only consisted sixty French divisions, three of which were only armoured, all much depleted. The Germans, however, were far superior in numbers and all their panzer divisions were intact, with little loss to men or material. A number of divisions too had time to halt and recoup before resuming its relentless drive west, ensuring that the troops fought efficiently and effectively at all times. The 7.Panzer-Division for instance after recouping in the Dunkirk area resumed its advance on 5 June, and drove for the River Seine to secure the bridges near Rouen. Advancing 62-miles in two days, the division reached Rouen, only to find the bridges destroyed. On 10 June Rommel reached the coast near Dieppe, sending his 'Am at coast' signal to the German HQ.

On 10 June Rundstedt's Army Group A was given the task of advancing south-wards in the direction of the Rhone Valley and the Alps, with the objective of cutting of the French armies to the east, while Army Group C was to move its forces at speed and destroy what was left of the enemy. It was here, in north-eastern France, that the Germans were ordered to ensure the ultimate collapse of the Maginot Line, and prevent the attempted withdrawal of enemy forces towards the south-west. German forces were also to prevent the enemy with-drawing from the Paris area, and those deploying themselves on the lower Seine were to establish a new front.

Horse drawn infantry cross a combination fixed-type bridge. A pioneer can be seen wading across the relatively shallow river in his inflatable bridge. Pioneer truppen were equipped with a number of these inflatable boats and infantry men could also use them.

Infantrymen with their horses rest in a field during a pause in their advance through northern France in late May 1940. The soldiers are outfitted with the standard German equipment and their armament is the Mauser 7.9mm Kar98k carbine, the standard issue Wehrmacht's shoulder weapon.

A pile of French artillery rounds still in their protected wooden slats for shipping lay abandoned on a road somewhere in northern France in late May 1940.

Armoured crewmen pause in their advance. One crewman jokes with his comrades and dons a British black bowler hat to ridicule his enemy's retreat through northern France. Most of the men are wearing their special black Panzer uniforms. The *Panzertruppen* were very distinctive from the German soldier wearing his field-grey service uniform. The colour of the uniform was specially dyed in black purely to hide oil and other stains from the environment of working with the armoured vehicles. The black Panzer uniform itself was made of high quality black wool, which was smooth and free of imperfections. The uniform comprised of a short black double-breasted jacket worn with loose fitting black trousers. The deeply double-breasted jacket was high waisted and was specially designed to allow the wearer to move around inside his often cramped vehicle with relative comfort. The trousers were designed to be loose also in order to enable the wearer plenty of movement.

An SS artillery crew with their 15cm sIG 33 artillery gun.(*schweres Infanterie Geschütz 33*) This was the standard German heavy infantry gun used in the Second World War. It was the largest weapon ever classified as an infantry gun in the world at that time.

A forward observation post and General Erwin Rommel, commander of the 7th Panzer Division, is seen on a field telephone in late May 1940. The 7th Panzer Division was one of the most successful divisions in the German arsenal in the Western Front campaign and covered vast distances in a short period of time. Rommel's Panzer force soon earned the name of the *Gespensterdivision* (Ghost/Phantom Division) because of its speed and the fact that not even the German High Command knew exactly where is was on the situation maps. Rommel had a 'lead from the front' attitude and would sometimes purposely cut communications with the High Command if wished not to be disturbed. Such behavior in the German Army was unknown, but Hitler saw such dilatory tactics as showing complete confidence in the Blitzkrieg concept. However, Rommel was criticized by staff for being difficult to contact and locate.

A Waffen-SS soldier moving towards the battle front in early June 1940. The rifleman wears the M1938 type camouflage smock in 'plane tree' material. This early smock was intended to be worn over the personal equipment but in practice most soldiers wore it over the smock. The equipment is that of a typical German infantryman with gas cape pouch worn on the lower part of the web strap. He is armed with the standard Karabiner 98K bolt action rifle and has two stick grenades tucked into his black leather belt. His rifle pouches can be seen attached to his belt. Note the rifle ammunition box being carried in his right hand.

A column of dejected French PoWs are being led along a railway line accompanied by German infantry. By early June 1940 wholesale surrenders were taking place all over north eastern France as the last remnants of the BEF lines collapsed.

A heavy Waffen-SS MG34 machine gun position preparing to be fired against an enemy target. The machine gun is being operated from its sustain fire mount which provided long-range and sustain fire from a fixed position.

A German bicycle unit has halted in a French village before resuming its march further west. Soldiers were themselves surprised by the rapid advance of its forces and felt in awe of the invisibility of its arsenal against the French. Note the French civilian holding two bottles of wine in his hand and probably taking full advantage of the invasion of his village by trying to sell them to the conquering troops.

German infantry and a machine gun crew advance through a field passing a burning farm building. A disinterested cow can be seen lying in the field and looks on whilst a machine gunner passes by holding an MG34 ammunition case and carrying a spare gun barrel over his shoulder.

Three photographs showing captured French soldiers. The top two photos have been taken in sequence showing French soldiers surrendering to a German unit. A 3.7cm PaK35/36 has been positioned on the road and the gunner's remain on constant vigilance manning their weapon as the soldiers walk passed into captivity.

A sign reads on a tree '*Vorsicht Minen*' (Caution Mines). Two vehicles have already succumbed to the mine field unknowingly and been destroyed as a result.

A Pz.Kpfw.I passes through a French town. Although the armoured spearheads on the Western Front had been a complete success, it was in France that the Pz.Kpfw.I was totally outmoded as a battle tank.

Here a column of Pz.Kpfw.III's advance along a road passing infantry on horseback. The primary task of the Pz.Kpfw.III was intended to fight other tanks. But although it was a well-built tank, in terms of armour, armament and mobility, it was not outstanding. However, on the Western Front in 1940 it proved it worth and was highly successful.

A variety of halftrack vehicles are seen spread out across a field. In the foreground is an Sd.Kfz.10 halftrack and in the back ground are Sd.Kfz.251 halftracks. The vehicles are purposely spaced apart to reduce the threat of an aerial attack on its armoured column.

A devastated town somewhere in northern France. By the extent of damage to the buildings the Luftwaffe have subjected the town to heavy bombing.

In the foreground is a stationary Pz.Kpfw.II whilst in the background are Pz.Kpfw.IV's and Pz.Kpfw.II's, motorcycles and support vehicles. The Pz.Kpfw.I and Pz.Kpfw.II represented the substantial majority among the Panzers fighting in the West.

A group of captured French colonial troops. Almost 400,000 colonial soldiers made up the French Army in 1940. Although badly trained and equipped they fought in southern France against Italian forces, and in the north against some of the most irrepressibly German troops. However, unlike the French the German regarded the colonials as second-class citizens and treated brutally and even executed.

194. Inside a French village a Pz.Kpfw.38(t) has fallen foul of enemy anti-tank projectile, which has brought the vehicle to a flaming halt. An anti-tank shell has penetrated the vehicles side with such considerable force it has immobilized it by blowing apart its track links. Black scorched marks over the wheels may have had an internal fire.

Two photographs showing Pz.Kpfw.38(t) advancing into action. The vehicle was armed with a 3.7cm cannon, known in German service as the KwK 37(t). It was a semi-automatic falling block weapon that fired AP shot muzzle velocity of 750 metres per second and could easily penetrated 3.2cm of French or British armour at 1,100 metres.

A column passes over a heavy Bruckengerat B bridge. Note the use of 50-foot pontoon bridges. These bridges could be erected in a very short time, but one of the most important factors pioneers took into consideration before their construction was finding a site with a suitable exit route.

Abandoned Renault R35 tanks are a grim reminder of the speed and efficiency of the German war machine as it swept mercilessly across northern France capturing or annihilating everything in its wake. Passing these French vehicles is a never ending stream of frightened and bewildered civilians trying to escape the fury of the German drive through France.

SS troops more than likely from the 'Das Reich' Division halted inside a destroyed town in northern France. On 4 June the SS-Verfügungs Division and other organizations prepared for the beginning of *Fall Rot* (Case Red), the plan developed by the German High Command to conquer the rest of France.

An unusual photograph showing an SS soldier, probably from 'Das Reich', sitting on a Donkey wearing a papier-mâché figure head with a bowler hat. His SS comrades can be seen laughing at the spectacle, which was more than likely undertaken to ridicule the British and French retreat.

An interesting photograph showing a German medic attending to injured captured British soldiers sometime in early June 1940. These PoWs were to spend the rest of the war incarcerated in prisoner camps across Germany.

A motorcycle unit has halted inside a decimated town during Case Red. During this early period of the war motorcyclists still rode into battle and dismounted to fight. However, even during the battle of France the Germans soon begun to realize how vulnerable their riders were to small-arms fire and booby traps.

The furious drive through France was often exhausting for the average German infantryman that had to trudge many miles on foot. In this photograph a soldier takes a well earned nap on a horse drawn wagon. Note the two rifles attached to the side of the wagon.

Captured British troops have hitched a lift on the engine deck of a panzer. Two motorcyclists wearing their distinctive green-grey waterproof rubberised motorcycle coats stand next to the vehicle.

Chapter Five

The End Comes

In northern France the front lines were shrinking, cracking slowly but surely under the massive German pressure. German units seemed to be progressing with an increased determination and vigour, convinced of their ability to crush the enemy before it could prepare a secondary line of defence. In an unparalleled armoured dash, some units had covered more than 50-miles in just twenty-four hours. For many German soldiers, it was an exhilarating dash, panzers bucketing across the countryside, meeting in some places only isolated pockets of resistance. Parties of fugitive French or half hearted counter-attacks on German

An infantryman stands in a French town and observes the destruction of the surrounding buildings and the twisted burnt out remains of a number of enemy vehicles.

Three photographs showing a column of support vehicles and motorcycle combinations passing through a destroyed French town. By the time Case Red was initiated the French Army were doomed. Dominated by increasing losses, French commanders in the field became sodden with defeatism. Their armies were in a pitiful shape. They had been broken up; their armour expended and little was left of the weak air force. As for the German Army they were now in the process of rounding-up the remnants of the French Army as it tried frantically moving from one position to another in order to try and escape its pending defeat.

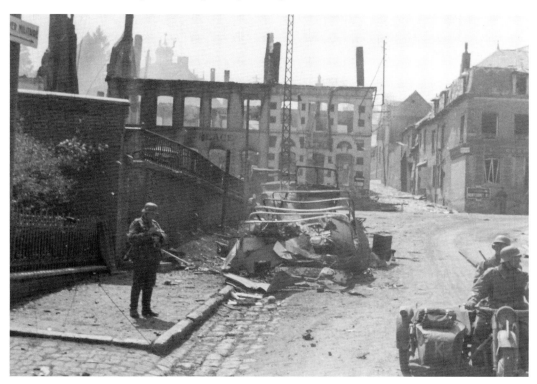

positions were ruthlessly cut down, although some of its remnants were able to escape across country. Many French troops seemed ready to surrender – some had even been seen tying handkerchiefs to their rifles coming out of decimated building or fox holes – yet there was no let up in the fighting. In some areas it was hard going for the German soldier and French positions occasionally stiffened and put up a heroic defence. However, the rate of the German thrust was greater than the French had anticipated. Militarily the French were doomed. Dominated by increasing losses, commanders in the field became sodden with defeatism. Their armies were in a pitiful shape. They had been broken up; their armour expended and little was left of the weak air force. Nevertheless, the French continued to fight with great bravery and tenacity, temporarily stopping even German armour, and standing-up resolutely to the incessant bombing of the Luftwaffe. But it was an unequal struggle. German troops inspired by their victorious gains, surged across France like a tidal wave, devouring the land as it marched.

In contrast among the greatest strains on all the German armies in France was the sheer length of the summer day. The advance had been so rapid, most commanding officers and their men found operations exhausting. As most soldiers on most days found themselves on the move or fighting fixed positions, they

Three photographs showing the extensive damage to a French city following a heavy Luftwaffe attack. During Case Red the Luftwaffe begun to limit its sorties against large towns and cities and proceeded to attack large enemy troop concentrations, bridges, the railway network and lines of communication.

Three photographs showing the endless columns of captured French troops trudging along a road. The Germans were prepared for very large numbers of prisoners following their experiences in Poland. In order to assist the huge quantities of prisoners being moved from the battlefront to the rear Order Police units were often deployed in assisting the efficient movement of the captured to the hastily erected PoW holding areas.

quickly adjusted to a routine and discovered that they could sleep on their feet, under bombardment, in their tanks, on the march.

By 14 June, the first German troops from the 9.Infantry-Division reported that they had arrived on the outskirts of Paris. Later that evening the division entered the French capital. Upon their arrival the Germans found to their surprise that much of the city had been evacuated with some 700,000 of the five million of the cities inhabitants remaining. The rest has taken to the roads south of the city, trying frantically in vain to escape the German drive. The French government, however, had earlier moved from Paris to the city of Tours. It then moved again to Bordeaux.

South of Paris all along the German front a succession of large and small-scale actions took place, driving vital wedges into the French defences. French strong-points were being knocked out either by superbly vigorous gunfire from tanks, or by determined action from infantry. The French Army was now being swamped by scores of German units, almost everywhere they had succeeded.

. Two Pz.Kpfw.II's advance along a congested road. Note the national flag draped on the engine deck of both vehicles for aerial recognition. The tanks are accompanied by motorcycle combinations, support vehicles, horse drawn infantry, an infantryman on a bicycle and a column of infantry vehicles. Note that each infantry vehicle possesses a bipod mount with an attached MG34 machine gun. Support vehicles were often issued with light machine guns for self-defence and a light weight anti-aircraft tripod 34.

Throughout the battle of France the strategic onus of ground movement laid totally with armour, and troops relied almost invariably upon it. The consequence was that the best armoured formations had to thrust forward again and again in the heart of the battle; losses were therefore inevitable. However, French tactics were shown to be not only unimaginative, but also unable to cope with the rapid speed in which events were constantly unfolding. There was nothing cowardly about the performance of the French Army, but there were simply overcome by the German tactics of blitzkrieg. Faced with the total collapse of their army, they continued to display sacrificial courage.

On 15 June von Kleists and Guderian's *panzergruppe* reported that their armour was now advancing at breakneck speed on both side of the Reims. These two powerful panzer groups caused massive problems to retreating enemy formations. Guderian's tanks successfully reached Bar0sur-Aube and Gray-sur-Saone, while armour of the von Kleist group had driven its armoured might into Saint-Florenetin and Tonnerre. Two days later, on 17 June, the right wing of Guderian's XXXIX Army Corps reached the Swiss border.

With the arrival of the German forces at the Swiss border a ring was closed around the remaining French troops who were now frantically withdrawing from

Two Pz.Kpfw.I's advance through a destroyed French town followed by support vehicles. The inhabitants of the town look-on as the German convoy passes through.

A motorcyclist leads a column of vehicles through a captured French town. On the opposite side of the road French civilians have packed their belongings and loaded them onto the roofs of their vehicles in order to escape to relative safety of family and friends either further west or to the south of France.

Lorraine and Alsace. Guderian was now able to move north-east and penetrate the Maginot fortifications from the rear using his powerful armoured units. In spite determined French resistance the Maginot Line, with its vast array of heavily constructed bunkers and well-armed fortifications, were soon overrun and captured. Troops that managed to flee from battle were normally spotted immediately by German reconnaissance aircraft and smashed by bombs and artillery directed from the air. The losses suffered by the infantry were then so heavy that impetus necessary to gather strength and hold a position was spent. Consequently, many soldiers entered the battle in low spirits at the thought of the enemy's enormous superiority.

In the final days just before the French Army finally capitulated, the Germans continued their advance, smashing the enemy. By the 20 June it was estimated that some 500,000 French soldiers had been captured. Large amounts of battlefield booty too fell into German hands.

To make the problems even greater for the French the Italians had declared war on the France sending some 32 divisions against some 6 French divisions.

However, against 185,000 troops the Italians made little progress against well-trained French soldiers of the Alps.

By 25 June 1940, some German spearheads had advanced as far as Lyon. Panzers were reported to be outside Bordeaux, and even inside Vichy. However, by this time the French government had already discussed with the a German delegation at Versailles that an armistice was to take effect sealing France's fate.

In total some 94,000 French soldiers had been killed in the battle for France and about a quarter of million injured. Almost two million French soldiers were taken prisoner by the Germans. By contrast, the German losses were much less, with 27,000 dead and 111, 000 wounded.

The battle of France had ended with another victory for the Germans. They had reaped the fruits of another dramatic Blitzkrieg campaign. France had proven ideal tank country to undertake a lightening war, and its conception seemed flawless. To many of the tacticians Blitzkrieg would ensure future victories.

Wehrmacht troops manhandling a 3.7cm PaK 35/36 gun down a river bank and onto what appears to be an inflatable boat. Ammunition boxes have been attached to the guns splinter shield. Note the French prisoners on the river bank watching the gun being transported.

Two photographs showing infantry honouring its dead in a French cemetery. Whilst the Germans lost far less troops during operations on the Western Front, some 27,000 soldiers were killed in the Low Countries and France.

„Sieg im Westen"

Ufaleih

Kriegsfilmbericht
des Heeres

31

Two Postcard
photographs taken in
sequence showing
mounted troops,
probably from a
reconnaissance
battalion of the
8.Infantry-Division
participate in the
victory parade
through Paris. In the
background is the
Arch of Triumph
(L'Arc de Triomphe
de l'Etoile).

The victory parade along the Avenue Foch on 16 June 1940. On the left a light cross-country car and on the right a Krupp LKW with a mounted MG34 machine for anti-aircraft protection and ground targets, both advance along the road passing a line of military spectators.

Soldiers from the 8.Infantry-Division rest beside a Parisian cafe with their rifles stacked and their machine guns resting on bipods. Their personal equipment has also been taken off and lay on the pavement.

A German checkpoint has been erected following the victory parade down the Avenue Foch. Security in the central district of Paris was tight, and checkpoints became a common feature for the Parisians that had to endure German occupation for the next four years.

During the early evening of 14 June 1940, the first German troops, men of the 9.Infantry-Division, entered Paris. Here in this photograph a number of light support and motorcycle combinations can be seen in front of the Eiffel Tower.

Three photographs showing Generalfeldmarschall Herman Goring, commander-in-Chief of the Luftwaffe, donned in his familiar new-style white summer tunic during his visit to Paris. It was Goring that had personally taken control of the Luftwaffe in the West, and had used its Blitzkrieg tactics with devastating effect. In front of both Luftwaffe and Wehrmacht commanders he perhaps felt with justification that his air force had played a decisive part in the success in the campaign.

A rifle company mach toward the main parade route in Paris. These soldiers are more than likely from the 9.Infantry-Division, which were the first troops to enter the French capital. The main ceremonial entry was made later in the day by elements of the 8.Infantry-Division.

During the victory parade in Paris and a German military band can be seen playing as German armour and infantry march along the Avenue Foch. A Pz.Kpfw.III command tank can be seen advancing along the road with French tanks following closely behind.

Order of Battle

German Army
OKH Reserve
German Second Army
5th Infantry Division
German Ninth Army
I Corps
XVII Corps
XXXVI Corps
XXXVIII Corps
XXXIX Corps
XLII Corps
XLIII Corps
German Army Group A
Commanded by Colonel General **Gerd von Rundstedt**
(Chief of Staff – Lt.Gen. Georg von Sodenstern)

German Fourth Army – Colonel General **Günther von Kluge**
(Chief of Staff – Maj.Gen. Kurt Brennecke)

II Corps – General of Infantry Carl-Heinrich von Stülpnagel
12th Infantry Division – Maj.Gen. Walther von Seydlitz-Kurzbach
31st Infantry Division – Lt.Gen. Rudolf Kämpfe
32nd Infantry Division – Lt.Gen. Franz Böhme

V Corps – General of Infantry Richard Ruoff
62nd Infantry Division – Maj.Gen. Walter Keiner
94th Infantry Division – Gen. of Infantry Hellmuth Volkmann
263rd Infantry Division – Maj.Gen. Franz Karl

VIII Corps – Gen. of Artillery Walter Heitz
8th Infantry Division – Lt.Gen. Rudolf Koch-Erpach
28th Infantry Division – Maj.Gen. Johann Sinnhuber

XV Corps – Gen. of Infantry Hermann Hoth
5th Panzer Division – Lt.Gen. Joachim Lemelsen -> 6.6.1940 Maj.Gen. Ludwig Cruwell
2nd Infantry Division (mot.) – Lt.Gen. Paul Bader
7th Panzer Division – Maj.Gen. Erwin Rommel

Reserves
87th Infantry Division – Maj.Gen. Bogislav von Studnitz
211th Infantry Division – Maj.Gen. Kurt Renner
267th Infantry Division – Lt.Gen. Ernst Fessman

German Twelfth Army – Colonel General **Wilhelm List**
(Chief of Staff – Lt.Gen. Eberhard von Mackensen)

III Corps – Gen. of Artillery Curt Haase
3rd Infantry Division – Lt.Gen. Walter Lichel
23rd Infantry Division – Lt.Gen. Walter von Brockdorff-Ahlefeldt
52nd Infantry Division – Lt.Gen. Hans-Jurgen von Arnim

VI Corps – Gen. of Engineer Wilhelm Förster
15th Infantry Division – Lt.Gen. Ernst Eberhard Hell
205th Infantry Division – Lt.Gen. Ernst Richter

XVIII Corps – Gen.of Infantry Eugen Beyer -1.6. Lt.Gen. Hermann von Speck
25th Infantry Division – Lt.Gen. Erich Heinrich Clössner
81st Infantry Division – Maj.Gen. Friedrich-Wilhelm von Löper
290th Infantry Division – Lt.Gen. Max Dennerlein -> 8.6.1940 Maj.Gen. Theodor Wrede

German Sixteenth Army- Gen. of Infantry **Ernst Busch**
(Chief of Staff – Maj.Gen. Walther Model)

VII Corps – Gen.Of Infantry Eugen von Schobert
16th Infantry Division – Maj.Gen. Heinrich Krampf
24th Infantry Division – Maj.Gen. Justin von Obernitz -> 1.6.1940 Maj.Gen. Hans-Valentin Hube
36th Infantry Division – Lt.Gen. Georg Lindemann
76th Infantry Division – Maj.Gen. Maximilian de Angelis
299th Infantry Division – Maj.Gen. Willi Moser

XIII Corps – Lt.Gen. Heinrich von Vietinghoff
17th Infantry Division – Lt.Gen. Herbert Loch
21st Infantry Division – Maj.Gen. Otto Sponheimer
160th Infantry Division – Maj.Gen. Otto Schunemann

XXIII Corps – Lt.Gen. Albrecht Schubert
73rd Infantry Division – Lt.Gen. Bruno Bieler
82nd Infantry Division – Maj.Gen. Josef Lehmann
86th Infantry Division – Maj.Gen. Joachim Witthöff
<u>**Reserves**</u>
6th Infantry Division – Lt.Gen. Arnold von Biegeleben
26th Infantry Division – Lt.Gen. Sigismund von Förster
71st Infantry Division – Lt.Gen. Karl Weisenberger

Panzer Group "Kleist" – Gen of Cavalry Paul Ludwig Ewald von Kleist
(Chief of Staff – Maj.Gen. Kurt Zeitzler)
XIV Corps – Gen. of Infantry Gustav Anton von Wietersheim
9th Infantry Division – Lt.Gen. Georg von Apell
13th Mot.Division – Maj.Gen. Friedrich-Wilhelm von Rothkirch
9th Panzer Division – Maj.Gen. Alfred Hubici
10th Panzer Division – Lt.Gen. Ferdinand Schaal
Infantry Regiment "Grossdeutschland" – Lt.Col. Gerhard von Schwerin

XXXXI Corps
2nd Motorised Division – Josef Harpe
Reserve
27th Infantry Division – Lt.Gen Friedrich Bergmann

German Army Group B
Commanded by Colonel General **Fedor von Bock**
(Chief of Staff – Lt.Gen. Hans von Salmuth).

German Sixth Army —Colonel General **Walter von Reichenau**
(Chief of Staff – Maj.Gen. Friedrich Paulus).

XVI Corps – Gen. of Cavalry Erich Hoepner
4th Infantry Division – Lt.Gen. Erich Hansen
33rd Infantry Division – Maj.Gen. Rudolf Sintzenich
3rd Panzer Division – Maj.Gen. Horst Stumpff
4th Panzer Division – Maj.Gen. Ludwig Radlmeier -> 8.6.1940 Maj.Gen. Johann

Joachim Stever IV Corps – Gen.of Infantry Viktor von Schwedler
15th Infantry Division – Maj.Gen. Ernst-Eberhard Hell
205th Infantry Division – Lt.Gen. Ernst Richter
XI Corps- Lt.Gen. Joachim von Kortzlesich
7th Infantry Division – Maj.Gen. Eccard von Gablenz
211th Infantry Division – Maj.Gen. Kurt Renner
253rd Infantry Division – Lt.Gen. Fritz Kuhne

IX Corps
XVI Corps
3rd Panzer Division
4th Panzer Division

XXVII Corps
German Eighteenth Army — Georg von Küchler
Reserves
208th Infantry Division
225th Infantry Division
526th Infantry Division
SS "Verfügungstruppe" Division
7th Airborne Division
22nd Air Landing Infantry Division
9th Panzer Division
207th Infantry Division

X Corps
SS "Adolf Hitler" Division
227th Infantry Division
1st Cavalry Division
XXVI Corps
256th Infantry Division
254th Infantry Division
SS "Der Führer" Division
German Army Group C
Commanded by Wilhelm Ritter von Leeb.
German First Army — Erwin von Witzleben

XII Corps
XXIV Corps
XXX Corps

XXXVII Corps

German Seventh Army — Friedrich Dollmann

Reserves

XXV Corps

XXXIII Corps

Italian Army Group "West"

Commanded by Prince General Umberto di Savoia

1st Army – General Pietro Pintor

2nd Corps – General Francesco Bettini

3rd Corps – General Mario Arisio

15th Corps – General Gastone Gambara

4th Army – General Alfredo Guzzoni

1st Corps – General Carlo Vecchiarelli

4th Corps – General Camillo Mercalli

Alpine Corps – General Luigi Negri

French Army

French 1st Army

French Cavalry Corps

2nd Light Mechanized Division

3rd Light Mechanized Division

French 3rd Corps

1st Moroccan Infantry Division

2nd North African Infantry Division

French 4th Corps

32nd Infantry Division

5th Corps

5th North African Infantry Division

101st Infantry Division

VII Corps

2nd Chasseurs Ardennais

8th Infantry Division

French 2nd Army

2nd Light Cavalry Division

5th Light Cavalry Division

1st Cavalry Brigade

French 10th Corps
3rd North African Infantry Division
5th Light Cavalry Division
55th Infantry Division
71st Infantry Division

French 18th Corps
1st Colonial Infantry Division
41st Infantry Division
French 7th Army

21st Infantry Division
60th Infantry Division
68th Infantry Division

French 1st Corps
1st Light Mechanized Division
25th Motorized Division

French 16th Corps
9th Motorized Division

French 9th Army
4th North African Infantry Division
53rd Infantry Division

French 2nd Corps
4th Light Cavalry Division
5th Motorized Division

French 11th Corps
1st Light Cavalry Division
18th Infantry Division
22nd Infantry Division

French 41st Corps
61st Infantry Division
102nd Fortress Division
3rd Spahi Brigade

British Expeditionary Force – General **Lord Gort**
5th Infantry Division
12th Infantry Division
23rd Infantry Division
46th Infantry Division

British I Corps – Lieutenant-General **Michael Barker** succeeded by Major-General **Harold Alexander**
1st Infantry Division
2nd Infantry Division
48th Infantry Division

British II Corps – Lieutenant-General **Alan Brooke** succeeded by Major-General **Bernard Montgomery**
3rd Infantry Division
4th Infantry Division
50th Infantry Division

British III Corps – Lieutenant-General **Ronald Adam**
42nd Infantry Division
44th Infantry Division

Belgian Army
Belgian I Corps
1st Infantry Division
4th Infantry Division
7th Infantry Division

Belgian II Corps
6th Infantry Division
11th Infantry Division
14th Infantry Division

Belgian III Corps
1st Chasseurs Ardennais
2nd Infantry Division
3rd Infantry Division

Belgian IV Corps
9th Infantry Division

15th Infantry Division
18th Infantry Division

Belgian V Corps
12th Infantry Division
13th Infantry Division
17th Infantry Division
Belgian VI Corps
5th Infantry Division
10th Infantry Division
16th Infantry Division

Belgian Cavalry Corps
1st Cavalry Division
2nd Cavalry Division

French Second Army Group
Maginot Line from Montmedy to south of Strasbourg, and controlled three armies.
French 3rd Army
3rd Light Cavalry Division
6th Infantry Division
6th North African Infantry Division
6th Colonial Infantry Division
7th Infantry Division
8th Infantry Division
French Colonial Corp
2nd Infantry Division
51st British Infantry Division
56th Infantry Division
French 6th Corp
26th Infantry Division
42nd Infantry Division
French 24th Corp
51st Infantry Division
French 42nd Corp
20th Infantry Division
58th Infantry Division

French 4th Army
1st Polish Infantry Division
45th Infantry division
French 9th Corp
11th Infantry Division
47th Infantry Division
French 20th Corp
52nd Infantry Division
82nd African Infantry Division

French 5th Army
Directly reporting:
44th Infantry Division
French 8th Corp
24th Infantry Division
31st Infantry Division
French 12th Corp
16th Infantry Division
35th Infantry Division
70th Infantry Division
French 17th Corp
62nd Infantry Division
103rd Infantry Division
French 43rd Corp
30th Infantry Division

French Third Army Group
French 3rd Army GroupMaginot Line, along the River Rhine and controlled a single army.

French 8th Army
French 7th Corps
13 Infantry Division
27 Infantry Division
French 13th Corps
19 Infantry Division
54 Infantry Division
104 Infantry Division
105 Infantry Division
French 44th Corps

67 Infantry Division
French 45th Corps
57 Infantry Division
63 Infantry Division

Dutch Army

Dutch I Corps
Dutch 1st Infantry Division
Dutch 3rd Infantry Division

Dutch II Corps
Dutch 2nd Infantry Division
Dutch 4th Infantry Division

Dutch III Corps
Dutch 5th Infantry Division
Dutch 6th Infantry Division

Dutch IV Corps
Dutch 7th Infantry Division
Dutch 8th Infantry Division
Dutch Light Division

Personal Equipment & Weapons

The German soldier was very well equipped and perhaps in 1939, when the German war was unleashed against Europe they were perhaps the best in the world. The rifleman or *Schütze* wore the trademark model 1935 steel helmet, which provided ample protection whilst marching to the battlefront and during combat. His leather belt with support straps carried two sets of three ammunition pouches for a total of 60 rounds for his carbine. The soldier also wore his combat harness for his mess kit and special camouflage rain cape or *Zeltbahn*. He also wore an entrenching tool, and attached to the entrenching tool carrier was the bayonet, a bread bag for rations, gas mask canister, which was invariably slung over the wearers shoulder and an anti-gas cape in its pouch attached to the shoulder strap. The infantryman's flashlight was normally attached to the tunic and inside the tunic pocket he carried wound dressings. A small backpack was issued to the soldiers, though some did not wear them. The backpack was intended for spare clothing, personal items, and additional rations along with a spare clothing satchel.

The weapons used by the German soldier varied, but the standard issue piece of equipment was the 7.92mm Kar98k carbine. This excellent modern and effective bolt-action rifle was of Mauser design. This rifle remained the most popular weapon used by the German Army throughout the war. Another weapon used by the German Army, but not to the extent used by the Kar98k, was the 9mm MP38 or MP40 machine pistol. This submachine gun was undoubtedly one of the most effective weapons ever produced for the German war machine. The 7.92mm MG34 light machine gun was yet another weapon that featured heavily within the ranks of the German Army. The effectiveness of the weapon made it the most superior machine gun ever produced at that time. The MG34 possessed a very impressive fire rate and could dominate the battlefield both in defensive and offensive roles. The German Army possessed the MG34 in every rifle group, and machine gun crews were able to transport this relatively light weapon easily onto the battlefield by resting it over the shoulder. Yet another weapon, which was seen at both company and battalion level on the battlefield, was the 5cm l.GrW36 light mortar and 8cm s. GrW34 heavy mortar. Although they could both be an effective weapon when fired accurately the light and heavy mortar was far too heavy and too expensive to produce on a very large scale.

At regimental and divisional level the German Army possessed its own artillery in the form of 7.5cm l.IG18, 10.5cm l.FH18, 15cm s. FH18, and 15cm s. IG33 infantry guns. Specially trained artillery crews used these guns and they were seen extensively in Poland, Western Front, Balkans, and the first two years of war in Russia. The 3.7cm Pak35/36 was another weapon that was very popular in 1940.

STANDARD GERMAN INFANTRY DIVISION

With the onset of war in the west the German infantry division had changed little from the assault divisions of 1918. The bulk of its supply and transport units were still by animal draught. The standard infantry rifle had basically not been changed since the war in the trenches, but its machine guns, notably the MG 34 and mortars were far superior to anything the enemy could muster. The artillery had changed little except that of the 10.5cm field howitzer, which had replaced the 7.7cm 18 infantry gun. Communication too was vastly superior to that of the enemy.

The Infantry division in 1939-41 averaged 16,860 men. This was made up of the following:

Officers: 518,
NCOs: 2,573
Other Ranks: 13,667
Officials: 102
Of the total standard infantry division only about 65% consisted of combat troops, the remainder were support elements of the division.

Three infantry regiments comprised of:

Officers: 75
NCOs: 493
Other Ranks: 2,474
Officials: 7

(Also included were staff and intelligence units)

Reconnaissance *(Aufklärungs)* **Battalion: 623 Officers and men**
Anti-tank *(Panzerjäger)* **Battalion: 550 Officers and men**
Engineer *(Pionier)* **Battalion: 520 Officers and men**
Artillery *(Artillerie*) **Regiment: 2,872 Officers and men**
Light *(Leichte)* **infantry 'column': 30 men**
Signal *(Nachrichten)* **Battalion: 474 Officers and men**
Supply services *(Versrgungsdienste)*: **226 Officers and men**
Logistics column / supply 'train' (3 motorised, 3 horse drawn): 180 Officers and men
Petrol, oil and lubricants column: 35 Officers and men
Workshop Company: 102 Officers and men
Transport Company: 245 Officers and men
Veterinary company: 235 Officers and men, 890 horses
2 Medical companies (1 Field Hospital and 2 medical transport platoons: 616 Officers and men

The infantry divisions also included the rations platoon, Bakery Company, butcher platoon, Military Police, and feldpost.